The Wildlife of

INCHKEITH

(A Comprehensive Record of the Birds, Mammals and Plants, associated with this famous Island in the middle of the Firth of Forth)

BY
RON MORRIS

Published by
Hillside
Scotland

Copyright © 2003 by Ron Morris

Published in Scotland in 2003
by Hillside

ISBN 0-9544760-0-X

All rights reserved. No part of this book may be reproduced or transmitted in any form or by any means, electronic or mechanical, including photocopying, recording, or by any information storage and retrieval system, without prior written consent from the Publisher.

Printed in Scotland by
David Macdonald Limited,
25 Rodney Street,
Edinburgh

Hillside
Hillside, Haughgate Street, Leven, Fife, Scotland, U.K. KY8 4SF

INTRODUCTION

Inchkeith lies in the Firth of Forth about four and a quarter miles north-north-east of Leith and three miles south-east of Kinghorn. At low tide the island is almost one mile long. It is a very irregularly shaped island, forming a rough triangle with north-east, north-west (East and West Stells) and south points.

The surface is very hilly, rising to 180' above sea level, and occupies over seventy acres. It is well vegetated with stoney beaches around much of its coastline and stretches of cliffs, particularly at the north-east and north-west points, and along the west side, including the harbour area. Some of the cliffs rise to over 100'.

Inchkeith has long been famous for its lighthouse, its 16th century French fort, of which very little now remains, and its military fortifications dating from the late 19th to mid 20th centuries. However, since the Second World War the island has also grown steadily in importance during the spring and summer months as a sanctuary for a variety of nesting seabirds. Despite this the island has not received the same degree of scrutiny from ornithologists, zoologists, or botanists, as have some of the other islands in the Firth of Forth, e.g. Isle of May, or Bass Rock, which has meant that much of its flora and fauna has gone uncharted. Even today there are a number of aspects of the island's natural history which have received no attention whatsoever, which is regrettable bearing in mind Inchkeith is the second largest island in the Firth of Forth.

Prior to the 1940's the only sea-faring bird species to nest on Inchkeith was the common eider duck. The island is now the main island stronghold in the Forth for northern fulmar, herring gull, and lesser black-backed gull, and also hosts sizable numbers of atlantic puffin, razorbill, great cormorant, european shag, and black-legged kittiwake, in addition to the common eider.

This document brings together information from a number of diverse sources which will hopefully afford a good insight into Inchkeith's natural history, as well as highlight the island's importance in this field.

LESSER BLACK-BACKED GULL

ACKNOWLEDGEMENTS

In compiling this record of Inchkeith's natural history, I am indebted to a number of people whose efforts and enthusiasm over the years have assisted me during many visits to the island. Amongst those who have been particularly helpful, are; the late Bob Smith, Betty Smith, Bill Bruce, Mike Ramage, Murray Wilson, Allan Murray, Douglas MacKean, George Ballantyne and Fife Nature. I am also conscious of my need to extend special thanks to Bill Simpson, loyal boatman, without whose great kindness and willingness to help my cause, much of the data contained herein would never have been gained. Also to Lynne Wilson who very kindly typed the initial draft of this document, and Jo Ballingall, who carried out the necessary proof-reading.

I must also extend my appreciation to Sir Tom Farmer, who via his secretary, and custodians of the island, has kindly granted permission for the island visits to take place.

VISITING INCHKEITH

There are no public landings at Inchkeith. Please note the island is "private property," owned by ORRMAC (810) Ltd. Due to past uses of the island, visiting Inchkeith is not recommended on the grounds of Health and Safety. All persons must carry their own personal insurance and indemnify the owners against accident, injury and death and this cover should be exhibited on demand to the owners.

Any enquiries should be made by telephoning the following number: 0131-315-2830

Cruises around the inner Forth islands can be arranged through Bill Simpson, owner of the Sea Hunter, who operates out of Granton harbour and a few other ports. He can be contacted via the following telephone numbers.

HOME :- 0131 - 538 - 9408

MOBILE :- 0777 - 410 - 3405

Trips around some of the inner Forth islands may also be arranged through Colin Aston ("Maid of the Forth Excursions").

Telephone Number :- 0131 - 331 - 4857

CONTENTS

Page

Introduction 3

Acknowledgements 4

Visiting Inchkeith 4

Birdlife
    Introduction 6
    List of Breeding Birds - Past and Present 8
    Historical Details of Inchkeith's Breeding Birds 9
    List of Non-breeding Birds Recorded from Inchkeith 23
    Historical Details of Non-breeding Birds Recorded from Inchkeith 25

Mammals 41

Butterflies 45

Flora 46

List of Flora recorded from Inchkeith 48

BIRDLIFE

Inchkeith's birdlife has been divided into two sections; "Breeding Birds - Past and Present" and "Other Birds recorded from Inchkeith". Thirty species are referred to in the first section and 101 species in the second. Where a species is covered by one section it is not referred to in the other. Wherever a species has been confirmed as having nested, or attempted to nest on the island, by way of an empty nest, nest with eggs or young, or recently fledged chicks, it will appear under the Breeding Birds section, otherwise it will automatically be included in the "Other Birds" section.

The following list of references have been used in compiling these sections.

Andrews; I.J. (1986) - The Birds of the Lothians
Cameron; W.A. (1957-60 and earlier records) - Birds at Inchkeith
Forth Seabird Group; (1994-2002) - Forth Island Bird Reports
Morris; R.A. (1988-2002) - Brief notes on Breeding Seabird Counts and other records
Ramage; M - Brief Records of Birdlife at Inchkeith
    (supplementing R.A. Morris's notes).
Rintoul; L.J. & Baxter, E.V. (1935) - A Vertebrate Fauna of Forth
Baxter; E.V. & Rintoul, L.J. (1953) - The Birds of Scotland
Sandeman; G.L.- Brief notes from several visits during the 1930's and 1950's
Sibbald; Sir R., Doctor of Medicine, (1710) - History of Fife and Kinross
Smith; R.W.J. (1959-95) - Brief notes on breeding seabird counts and other records.

Many of Baxter and Rintoul's records were based on information supplied by lightkeepers stationed at Inchkeith during the earlier part of the 20th century. Cameron himself was a lightkeeper stationed at the island between the years 1957-60. He has left us with the best all year round record study of birdlife at Inchkeith. However, his notes are now well out of date as there have been many changes since his time, more especially in the variety and numbers of breeding seabirds at the island.

Sandeman made a small number of visits during the 1930's and 1950's, and even spent a few months on Inchkeith during the latter part of 1939, during which time he made brief, but valuable notes on the island's birdlife which have helped to bridge the gap between Baxter and Rintoul's earlier references and Cameron's records.

R.W.J. Smith began monitoring the numbers of breeding seabirds on the islands in the Firth of Forth in 1959. This practice has been continued every year since, and more recently has been carried out by members of Forth Seabird Group, who produce an annual report in respect of each year's results. Although these counts are usually limited to a single day visit to each island each year, they have proved invaluable in mapping out the colonisation, increase, fluctuations and variety, of the breeding seabirds on the islands.

Since 1988 Smith's records for Inchkeith have been augmented by R.A. Morris, who is a member of the Forth Seabird Group and has made several visits to the island each year, accompanied by a variety of volunteers.

It will be appreciated that the small number of visits made each year, together with their brief nature, lends considerable scope to oversight and under-recording.

Baxter and Rintoul (Vertebrate Fauna of Forth, 1935) stated "Inchkeith was no doubt, in old days, a good island for birds, but the fortifications, the lighthouse, the horn, the wireless signalling station, have changed the face of the island so much that few birds breed here".

I have been unable to trace any records from the "old days" other than Dr. Sibbald's brief reference, but in pre-military days there were few buildings, and the island would have had a lusher growth of vegetation. The lightkeepers then, had one or two fields in which they kept domestic stock which would have attracted some of the bird species normally found on farmland to the island's shores.

Today there are even fewer small birds found on Inchkeith during the summer months, than were found a few decades ago. This is most likely due to the presence of nesting gulls which have imposed themselves over the whole of the island's surface during the breeding season. It may also be the case that climate changes, or even the national decline of some species, has had some effect.

Baxter and Rintoul in their references, have quoted a number of birds as occurring, or having bred on "some of the Forth islands" but where these references have not made specific mention of Inchkeith, they have largely been ignored.

As a result of recent changes made by the British Ornithologist's Union's Records Committee, to the common names of many of our bird species for the purpose of standardisation, it was considered prudent to adopt these changes for the relevant species covered by this booklet. Although many people may be unfamiliar with these new names, in most cases the changes are not so different in character that they would cause undue confusion.

ATLANTIC PUFFINS

LIST OF BREEDING BIRDS - PAST & PRESENT

Northern Fulmar
Great Cormorant
European Shag
Mallard
Common Eider
Common Shelduck
Greylag Goose
Eurasian Oyster Catcher
Great Black-backed Gull
Lesser Black-backed Gull
Herring Gull
Black-legged Kittiwake
Razorbill
Common Guillemot
Atlantic Puffin
Rock Pigeon/Feral Pigeon
Sky Lark
Barn Swallow
Carrion Crow
Winter Wren
Song Thrush
Common Blackbird
European Robin
Hedge Accentor
Meadow Pipit
Rock Pipit
Common Starling
Common Linnet
Reed Bunting
House Sparrow

RAZORBILL

BLACK-LEGGED
KITTIWAKE

HISTORICAL DETAILS OF INCHKEITH'S BREEDING BIRDS

NORTHERN FULMAR *Fulmarus glacialis*
The northern fulmar was first recorded from Inchkeith by Sandeman on 16th June 1934. However it did not take up residence at the island until during the Second World War.

In 1942 two pairs were present and by 1945 five nest sites were occupied. Three years later the population had risen to thirty occupied nest sites.

Numbers continued to increase over the years and a count in 1959, returned one hundred and five occupied nest sites. Thereafter northern fulmar numbers at Inchkeith continued to increase at a rate of about 7% per annum, reaching a peak of 656 nest sites in 1986!

Since then their numbers have fluctuated, dropping to 332 occupied nest sites in 1998, but recovering slightly to 419 in 2002.

Cameron found that by the end of the second week in September nearly all of the birds had left the cliffs, with 19th September being the latest date he recorded any, apart from 22nd October 1957. Cameron also found that birds returned to the cliffs during late November, or early December, with 15th November (1959) being his earliest recorded date for their return.

Northern fulmar numbers at Inchkeith have increased considerably since Cameron's time, and the island is now the most important site for this species in the Firth of Forth, after Tantallon cliffs in East Lothian.

GREAT CORMORANT *Phalacrocorax carbo*
Great cormorants have probably always roosted on Inchkeith's rocks and skerries. Dr. Sibbald (1710) stated that both the bigger (great cormorant) and the lesser sort (european shag), frequent its rocks. Sandeman recorded them regularly between 17th September and 19th November during 1939.

Cameron noticed they were present throughout the year, usually on the rocks to the south and west of the island, with between one and two hundred birds occasionally assembling during the winter months.

The great cormorant is a very recent breeding species at Inchkeith, first nesting on Long Craig reef just off the southern tip of the island in 1992. Eighteen nests were found, fourteen of which contained eggs and chicks.

Since then, the colony has built up steadily. In 1994 some birds nested for the first time on the southern point of mainland Inchkeith. The following year the whole colony had moved to this new site and contained 112 nests.

Although only seventy-five nests were estimated in 1998, 102 were recorded in 2002, with fifty-three of these being found on Long Craig and forty-nine at the mainland colony.

The number of breeding pairs of great cormorants at colonies can vary considerably from year to year, as the birds have a tendency to move about from one colony to another. Therefore, true population trends can only be gauged by taking into account the numbers of breeding birds at all the other colonies in the area.

Currently, the breeding great cormorant population in the Forth Estuary varies between 350 - 500 pairs.

EUROPEAN SHAG   *Phalacrocorax aristotelis*

Dr. Sibbald (1710) stated that both types of cormorant (great cormorant and european shag) frequented Inchkeith's rocks. Sandeman regularly recorded european shags at Inchkeith between 17th September and 19th November during 1939.

During the late 1950's european shags were regularly present, roosting in varying numbers, sometimes reaching about two hundred. A visit to the island on 4th January 1984 recorded 120 shags.

The first notification of a breeding attempt occurred in 1965 when an empty nest was found. However, it was not until 1974 that a pair bred successfully. Six pairs nested in 1977 and until the early 1980's, breeding numbers of european shags remained at between three and six pairs.

Thereafter the breeding population rose steadily to a peak of thirty nests in 1991, before the bad winters of 1992 and 1993 (which were particularly disastrous for this species) caused european shag numbers to dramatically decline. Only ten pairs attempted to nest in 1994, but by 1997 numbers had recovered with twenty-five pairs nesting. A survey on 29th June 2000, saw a marked rise to fifty-eight nests, almost double the previous peak figure.

Numbers of nesting european shags have continued to rise rapidly with 104 nests recorded on 1st June 2002.

MALLARD   *Anas platyrhynchos*

Four birds were recorded on 26th October 1939. A drake was seen on 21st December 1957 and a duck on 2nd November 1958.

Over the years since then, small numbers of mallard have been recorded on a number of occasions, particularly during the breeding season. Single nests were discovered in 1971 and 1976. In 1990 a nest containing eleven eggs, and a duck with a solitary duckling were recorded. Single nests were also recorded during the years 1991-94 and 1997-1998. Single broods of newly hatched ducklings were recorded on 23rd April and 10th July 1999. On 1st June 2002 a nest with nine eggs was discovered and, a second nest was suspected, but not found on 29th of that month.

Whilst the breeding population is low, nesting has probably taken place during most years over the last few decades. Seventy-two mallard were present at the island on 4th January 1984.

Unusually high numbers of mallard were present on 17th June 1979 (i.e. eighteen drakes and five ducks), 14th June 1981 (i.e. forty-one drakes and two ducks) and 4th January 1984 (seventy-two birds).

COMMON EIDER   *Somateria mollissima*

Common eider occur off Inchkeith during every month of the year, but from October to March numbers are usually small.

Sandeman recorded them in June 1934 and 1936 and single birds on odd days between 17th September and 19th November 1939, with twelve present on 25th September. He also noted three females offshore on 6th July 1951 and four-five on 2nd August.

Cameron noticed flocks of forty - sixty birds sheltering close inshore during stormy weather. His highest figure was 380 on 10th February 1960. He regularly saw flocks of 100 or more, during May or June.

The common eider is the bird for which we have the earliest breeding record for Inchkeith. In 1684 Sibbald stated that dunter goose's (common eider) eggs were found on the Isle of Keith (Inchkeith). However Baxter and Rintoul (Vertebrate Fauna of Forth -1935) state there was no recent record of nesting.

Eight nests were found in 1957, followed by twenty-seven in 1960. Since then breeding numbers have increased considerably with at least 323 nests accounted for in 1994.

On 6th May 1996 140 nests were recorded but this was a cursory count conducted early in the breeding season. On 2nd June of the same year, 535 birds were counted close inshore.

A duck ringed as an adult at the Farne Islands on 8th June 1959 was caught asleep on the rocks of Inchkeith on 24th February 1960. Twenty birds were recorded at the island on 4th January 1984 and c.250 were present on 15th November 2002.

COMMON SHELDUCK   *Tadorna tadorna*

There is only one breeding record for this species. In 1960 a pair nested in an old trench and hatched out nine ducklings. Other records for this species are: four birds offshore on 20th June 1962, one bird seen flying from the island onto the sea on 19th June 1963, one - two adults offshore on 15th June, 1969, one pair offshore on 14th June 1970, a drake offshore on 15th June 1997, one pair seen flying in to the island on 1st June 2002 and two individuals present on 6th July that year.

There is little doubt the common shelduck has bred at other times but have remained undiscovered due to their habit of nesting under rocks or down burrows.

GREYLAG GOOSE   *Anser anser*

Cameron recorded geese of "uncertain species" during 1959. On 8th February fifty-five were flying north-eastwards during dense fog, and on 25th and 27th October flocks of sixty-nine and one hundred respectively, were flying southwards. However, these birds were not associating with the island.

A pair of greylag geese (feral) were witnessed with two small goslings during June 1980 and one or two pairs have tried to breed during most years since, until very recent years.

Six pairs were present at the island in 1987 when at least three of these attempted to breed. These birds most likely originated from feral colonies in the Lothians or Beveridge Park, Kirkcaldy.

They were last confirmed as breeding on Inchkeith during 1996 when one pair nested. There was no evidence of them breeding in 1997. An unconfirmed report suggests a pair nested early in the breeding season of 1999, with a further pair also present. A single adult was also recorded in the harbour on 29th May that year.

Some unusual locations have been chosen for nest sites, e.g. the turfed roof of an old pill box; inside an old oil drum lying on its side (two years in succession) and, inside a small brick building.

EURASIAN OYSTER CATCHER *Haematopus ostralegus*

Occurs during all months of the year. During the 1950's Cameron regularly recorded flocks of between thirty - fifty during the winter months.

Two pairs were present during the breeding season in 1962, including a pair with a single chick. Breeding has probably been attempted every year since.

Numbers have slowly risen to between seven and ten pairs in recent years, with two or three nests normally discovered during most annual seabird monitoring visits.

On 4th January 1984 170 eurasian oyster catchers were recorded at the island and a visit on 10th November 2001 found over fifty birds roosting or feeding. About forty were noted on 15th November 2002.

GREAT BLACK-BACKED GULL *Larus marinus*

The great black-backed gull is one of the bird species Dr. Sibbald, recorded as frequenting Inchkeith's rocks in 1710. Sandeman saw up to fifty at a time between 17th September and 19th November 1939. Cameron recorded it throughout the year and noticed numbers increased during late August. He made regular counts of between 50-100 birds, with occasional counts of up to 200. These birds remained in numbers until February, but during March and April only very small numbers were present. About ten birds were recorded on 15th November 2002.

Breeding was confirmed for the first time in June 1995, when a pair was discovered with three chicks. The following month a second pair was discovered, the activities of which indicated breeding, but no nest or chicks were found.

Between fifteen - twenty-five birds were present on 6th November 1995.

Two pairs nested in 1996 and 1997, with possibly a third pair present. Single nests were recorded in 1998, 2001 and 2002.

LESSER BLACK-BACKED GULL *Larus fuscus*

This migratory species begins to arrive at the island in March with the bulk of the population turning up in April or early May. By early October they have all left. They are on record as being present at Inchkeith on 16th June 1934 and 2nd August 1951. Nesting was first confirmed in 1956 when two pairs bred and their numbers increased rapidly over ensuing years. In 1987 the population was estimated at about 1,753 nesting pairs and a large gull survey in 1994 returned an approximate figure of 2,607 pairs, an increase of 49% over the previous survey.

HERRING GULL *Larus argentatus*

This species is present throughout the year. Dr. Sibbald (1710) listed it as one of those species which frequented Inchkeith's rocks in his time. Sandeman recorded them in June 1934 and 1936 and also during his stay on the island from September - November 1939.

The first breeding attempt took place in 1940 and by 1958 numbers had increased to 319 nesting pairs. Over the ensuing years the herring gull, and lesser black backed gull, steadily colonised the whole of Inchkeith during the summer months, turning it into the largest gullery in the Forth estuary. In 1987 the breeding population of herring gull was estimated at 4,091 pairs and in 1994 a further survey estimated 4,977 nesting pairs.

Out-with the breeding season Cameron found them to be present in widely varying numbers, i.e. from less than fifty to more than 1,000. On 17th March 1960 he estimated at least 2,000 adult birds were present and on 3rd May the same year, he calculated that over 1,200 immature birds were on the south reef alone.

The breeding population nowadays is considerably greater than during Cameron's time and this may have a bearing on numbers at times out-with the breeding season, although the same "widely varying numbers" principle still seems to apply.

Breeding birds begin to arrive at the island in February and March and leave by the end of September.

Visits to the island out-with the breeding season recorded 1,000 birds on 4th January 1984, forty-sixty adult and immature birds on 6th November 1995, over 100 birds on 10th November 2001, and about 250 birds on 15th November 2002.

BLACK-LEGGED KITTIWAKE *Rissa tridactyla*

Sandeman recorded black-legged kittiwakes from Inchkeith in June 1934 and 1936, September - November 1939, and in July and August 1951.

Cameron recorded them during every month of the year but made very few records from December to March, during which time he saw mainly single birds and not more than four in a day. In the autumn he regularly saw flocks of between 100 - 400, noting a clear dispersal in early November.

However, these observations pre-date the establishment of the black-legged kittiwake as a breeding bird at the island.

In 1960 a pair built a nest, but no eggs were laid. Breeding was confirmed the following year, when a single pair nested. Following this their numbers increased rapidly to 407 pairs by 1971.

The species then declined as a breeding bird to 195 pairs in 1981, but numbers recovered afterwards to reach a new peak of 678 nesting pairs in 1992. Since then their numbers have fluctuated, with 440 pairs nesting in 1994, 551 pairs in 1995, 309 pairs in 2001, and 351 pairs in 2002.

RAZORBILL   *Alca torda*

Dr. Sibbald (1710) stated that "in the summer vast numbers of young marrots (razorbills) are catched in the sea about Inchkeith." These birds likely originated from May Island and Bass Rock, being attracted to Inchkeith's waters by the large amounts of fish which were reputedly found in the area at that time.

The next notification of this species is from Sandeman, who recorded the razorbill on the sea off Inchkeith in June 1936. Cameron recorded it every month of the year, but more-so during the winter months, with five being his optimum figure for a day on 24th January 1960. His observations, however, pre-date the establishment of the razorbill as a regular breeding bird at Inchkeith.

Razorbills were seen more frequently in the vicinity of the island during the breeding seasons of the 1960's.

In 1969 a pair took up territory in an empty kittiwake nest, but it was not until the following year that breeding took place, when two pairs were recorded nesting.

Razorbill numbers have steadily increased since then, reaching a peak of seventy-five nesting sites in 1998. In 2002 sixty-one nest sites were counted.

Razorbill numbers will always be restricted by the lack of suitable nesting sites at Inchkeith.

Three birds were recorded offshore on 4th January 1984, and "several" were seen offshore on 10th November 2001.

COMMON GUILLEMOT   *Uria aalge*

Sandeman recorded the common guillemot from the sea off Inchkeith in June 1936 and again in August 1951.

Cameron noted it every month of the year with up to eight in a day during August – September and also on 18th May 1960. Over his four year stay at Inchkeith he recorded over 300 common guillemots, of which only six were of the bridled form. As with some other species, his common guillemot observations pre-date the establishment of the species as a breeding bird at the island.

Common guillemots were seen offshore more frequently during the breeding seasons of the 1960's, but the first breeding did not take place until 1976 when a single pair was recorded.

As the compact nesting behaviour of common guillemots makes it difficult to assess the number of actual breeding pairs, the population of common guillemots is calculated in "individual birds" present on the cliffs on the date(s) counts are made.

Between forty-two and eighty-one birds have been counted in most recent years, but on 15th June 1997 106 birds were noted. However, only twenty-seven birds were present on the cliffs (mainly in the harbour area) on 1st June 2002.

Breeding common guillemot numbers will always be very limited at Inchkeith, due to a lack of suitable nesting ledges for this species.

A bird washed up dead on 27th September 1959 had been ringed as an adult bird at the Isle of May on 16th July 1958. Fourteen birds were recorded offshore on 4th January 1984 and two were close inshore on 15th November 2002.

ATLANTIC PUFFIN   *Fratercula arctica*

Cameron recorded between one and six birds offshore on different dates between 15th June and 17th July 1960. His only other records were of occasional dead birds washed ashore in winter. On 6th September 1959, one bird which was washed up had been ringed as an adult at Luroy Island, north-west Norway, on 9th July 1956.

A single bird was seen onshore, and a further five offshore, on 14th June 1961. Breeding was first confirmed in 1965 when one nest was found. Ten birds were recorded in the vicinity of the island on the same date.

Because of the atlantic puffin's habit of nesting down burrows, it is very difficult to assess actual breeding numbers, especially for an island the size of Inchkeith. Over the years the island's atlantic puffin population has been given in the total number of birds seen onshore and offshore, on a single day during the breeding season, which is a highly erratic and inaccurate way of assessing breeding puffin populations. However, carried out year after year, this method can at least show general trends in population over a period of time.

In 1978 1,000 birds were counted. This figure trebled in 1991, but in 1995 the count was down to about 1,200 birds.

Just to emphasize how populations of atlantic puffin can vary considerably at a colony on two separate dates within the same breeding season, on 25th May 1997 870 birds were recorded at Inchkeith, whilst a repeat count on 15th June returned a minimum of 3,209 birds.

Rough estimates of the current breeding population vary between 1,500 and 3,000 pairs. On 1st June 2002, over 1,305 birds were counted. A completely "white" atlantic puffin was observed close inshore to the east side of Inchkeith on 10th July 1987. However it wasn't established if this bird was a true albino or not.

ROCK PIGEON / FERAL PIGEON   *Columba livia*

During his time at Inchkeith, Cameron recorded four possible sightings of single rock doves. The purity of this species must always be questioned due to the frequent inter-breeding with feral doves. However both forms are now classed as rock pigeon.

As rock/feral pigeons are most usually ignored by "serious" bird watchers it is not clear when they first started to breed at Inchkeith. Most likely this took place some time after Cameron's departure as he never recorded it.

The rock/feral pigeon is now a very common breeding bird at the island, building its nest in the old military buildings and fortifications, as well as down rabbit and puffin burrows and under rocks.

In 1997 it was recorded as numerous and breeding. On 10th November 2001 over 1,000 rock/feral pigeons were present at Inchkeith.

SKY LARK   *Alauda arvensis*

A number of sky larks were recorded as singing in June 1934 and as being present two years later.

Up to ten were recorded at all times between 17th September and 19th November 1939 and in July 1951 two or three birds were seen, one of them singing. From these observations it may be reasonably assumed the sky lark was a breeding bird at Inchkeith over this period. However, Baxter and Rintoul (Birds of Scotland - 1953) stated "The sky lark does not breed on any of the islands in the Forth except Cramond Island".

One or two pairs bred at Inchkeith every year between 1957-1960. Cameron noticed they arrived at the island about mid-February and remained throughout the summer. He also noticed a small passage during the autumn.

There are no records since Cameron's time.

BARN SWALLOW   *Hirundo rustica*

Baxter and Rintoul (Vertebrate Fauna or Forth, 1935) stated the barn swallow occurred as a passage migrant at Inchkeith. Sandeman saw two or three birds between the dates 17th September and 8th October 1939.

In Birds of Scotland (1953) Baxter and Rintoul stated the only Forth island on which it has bred was Cramond Island. However Cameron recorded it as breeding on Inchkeith every year between 1956-60 and said it may have done so previous to that.

One pair nested on the island each year between 1956-58, two - three pairs in 1959, and three pairs in 1960.

Most nests were constructed in old army huts, many of which have since disappeared. Small numbers of birds were recorded during a number of breeding seasons up to the late 1970's, so breeding may have continued beyond Cameron's time.

Cameron noted barn swallows first arrived at the island about mid-February and also noticed a small passage during the autumn. Recent records include two birds present on 2nd May 1994, three on 6th May and one on 2nd June 1996.

CARRION CROW   *Corvus corone*

Sandeman recorded a single bird at the island during a visit on 25th October 1934 and Cameron recorded it in every month of the year, with one or two adults seen at a time and up to four on occasion.

The carrion crow first attempted to breed in 1957, but was unsuccessful, and a later nest built in 1960, succumbed to a strong wind. An empty nest was also found in 1968.

There have probably been breeding attempts during most years since at least 1975, with some of them being successful. Two nests containing four and five eggs respectively, were discovered on 3rd May 1993 but on 6th June both nests were seen to have failed. A third nest (new), which was empty, was found on the same date.

The following year two nests successfully fledged young and, in 1995 three nests were discovered after the crow's nesting season. Two of the three nests were found to be empty as expected, but the third nest contained two small chicks, which were dead.

On 6th May 1996 two nests were noted, one containing four feathered chicks, whilst the other was out of reach, having been constructed on the walkway of the lighthouse tower.

Single nests containing chicks were recorded in 1997 and 1998 and a recently fledged juvenile was found in a derelict building on 1st June 2002.

Three birds were recorded at the island on 4th January 1984.

WINTER WREN   *Troglodytes troglodytes*

Baxter and Rintoul (Vertebrate Fauna of Forth, 1935) stated they had a good many autumn and winter records for this species and Sandeman recorded it regularly between 17th September and 19th November 1939.

Cameron noticed the winter wren was present in increased numbers over the autumn and winter periods, but not more than thirteen or fourteen, except on 31st October 1960, when he counted twenty-six.

A small number probably breed in most years. Young fledged from single nests in 1958 and 1960. During the latter year, two further empty nests were found and a separate adult was seen carrying food.

Birds have been seen or heard most breeding seasons since the 1960's and occasionally nests have been found. At least three empty nests were found in 1992, but some of these could have been a year or two old, their condition preserved by being located within old military buildings. Two further empty nests were discovered in 1994, one of them in new condition.

Recent records include one or two birds singing on 10th June 1995, fifteen birds on 6th November the same year, a single bird seen on 6th May 1996, twelve birds on 4th January, 1984, a single bird on 10th July, 1999, "several" on 10th November 2001, and "many" birds present on 15th November 2002.

SONG THRUSH   *Turdus philomelos*

Baxter and Rintoul (Vertebrate Fauna of Forth, 1935) reported "rushes" of song thrushes at Inchkeith on 6th August 1913 and 11th August 1914. They also reported great rushes of the "continental race" on 21st September, 9th October, 22nd - 30th October and 5th November 1912.

Sandeman recorded small numbers present in June 1934 and 1936, 17th September - 19th November 1939, July and August 1951, and again in July 1955. No doubt the song thrush was breeding over this span of years. It bred every year between 1957 - 1960, with Cameron counting thirty-one nests during this time, including five in 1957, eleven in 1958 and nine in 1960. One nest was discovered in 1964 and in 1968 an adult was seen feeding fledged young.

In Cameron's time very few song thrushes occurred during the winter, with only one or two birds being present on any given day. He did notice a small autumn passage comprising between twelve - fifteen birds at the most.

The only records since Cameron's time are of individual birds seen on 18th May 1975, 4th January 1984, 2nd May 1990, and 10th November 2001. An old nest was found inside a disused building in 1994, but this could have been of several years' vintage. At least eight birds were present on 15th November 2002.

COMMON BLACKBIRD   *Turdus merula*

Baxter and Rintoul (Vertebrate and Fauna of Forth, 1935) stated that passages of blackbirds had been recorded from Inchkeith.

Cameron recorded common blackbirds on passage each year during October - November, when flocks of between fifteen - twenty-five occurred. On 21st October 1960, during poor visibility and following an easterly gale, he counted a flock of forty-one birds. He also saw flocks of between fifteen - twenty birds in January.

Sandeman found the common blackbird breeding on 16th June 1934, and stated many were present between 27th - 28th June 1936. He also recorded them regularly between 17th September - 19th November 1939 and, in July and August 1951 he noted small numbers.

The common blackbird bred every year between 1957-60, although their population declined from ten pairs in the former year, to just two pairs in the latter year. Nevertheless, there have probably been attempts at breeding every year since, as one or two birds are recorded each breeding season, and occasionally their nests have been found. In 1975 it was estimated that between five and ten pairs nested.

More recently, in 1994 four males and three females were recorded, along with a nest containing three eggs. Three nests were found in buildings on 6th May 1996, and two were found, again in buildings, on 15th June 1997. One - two birds are normally seen during a visit to the island, and the common blackbird most likely continues as a breeding bird at Inchkeith.

At least thirty birds were recorded on 15th November 2002.

EUROPEAN ROBIN   *Erithacus rubecula*

Baxter and Rintoul (Vertebrate Fauna of Forth, 1935) stated that probably the greatest immigrations recorded in October and November are of the continental redbreast.

Birds which were present on 16th August 1912 appeared to be of the British variety, whilst those which occurred in October 1912 and 1914 appeared to be of the continental race.

Sandeman recorded two birds on the island between 24th September and 19th November 1939. Cameron made many records between 22nd August and 21st March, during the years of his stay, but numbers never exceeded three or four, except during a four day period near the end of October 1960, when between seven and nine birds were present. Nine birds were also recorded on 4th January 1984.

On 20th March 1989, Morris caught a european robin by torchlight whilst exploring an underground magazine at the west fort. Another bird was seen on 2nd May 1994.

Attempts at breeding are assumed from four empty european robin type nests found in 1992 (north battery), 1994 (south battery), 1996 and 1997 (both west battery).

At least two birds were present on 10th November 2001, and a large "fall" of this species was recorded on 15th November 2002.

HEDGE ACCENTOR (Hedge Sparrow or Dunnock)   *Prunella modularis*

The hedge accentor is reported to have nested in 1912. It was present on the island in "numbers" on 1st November 1913. Baxter and Rintoul (Birds of Scotland, 1953) stated "It has bred on Inchkeith where it appears to be a summer visitor as the breeding birds were said to return in March".

Cameron recorded up to six present throughout the year.

A pair may have nested in 1959 when an adult bird was seen carrying food. The following year two pairs raised four birds each.

No doubt the hedge accentor has nested in other years, but its secretive nature and drab colour make it all too easy to overlook. An individual was recorded on 19th June 1963.

MEADOW PIPIT   *Anthus pratensis*

Baxter and Rintoul (Vertebrate Fauna of Forth, 1935) had records for both spring and autumn passage.

Sandeman recorded the meadow pipit as present on 16th June 1934 and one pair as nesting on 27th-28th June 1936. He reported them as common and "probably with young" on 6th July 1951. On 2nd August of that year he counted twenty-three birds.

Cameron also recorded some birds on spring passage, but with more occurring in the autumn. Smith reported the meadow pipit as apparently breeding on 3rd June 1959. The following year Cameron recorded at least seven, with probably ten pairs breeding. They may also have bred during 1969.

Four birds were seen during the breeding season of 1975 and a single bird was recorded in May 1979. Another four were noted on 2nd May 1994 and at least eight were present on 15th November 2002.

ROCK PIPIT   *Anthus petrosus*

Sandeman recorded the Rock Pipit in June 1934 and 1936 and regularly between 17th September and 19th November 1939. On 6th July 1951 he noted it as "common, probably with young" and in August of that year he recorded it as "plentiful with fully fledged young". It was also present in July 1955.

Cameron reported it as breeding each year between 1957-60 with between five and seven pairs nesting during the latter year. He also noted it was present throughout the year, with up to ten birds occurring in mid-winter.

Since Cameron's time, small numbers were seen each breeding season until the late 1970's, there-after only one or two birds have been encountered during annual seabird monitoring visits.

On 2nd June 1996 two individual birds in separate territories, were witnessed carrying food and, on 15th June 1997 individual birds were reported from three separate locations. Four birds were noted on 4th May 1998, one of which was carrying nesting material into a crevice in the west cliffs. On 6th June the same year, four birds were again recorded and three territories were "suspected". Four - five birds were noted on 29th May the following year.

Out-with the breeding season, nineteen birds were counted during a visit to the island on 4th January 1984 and over twelve birds were present on 10th November 2001.

COMMON STARLING   *Sturnus vulgaris*

Sandeman recorded the common starling in June 1934 and 1936 and also regularly between 17th September and 19th November 1939. He also recorded a flock of over 100 on 6th July and between fifty - seventy on 2nd August 1951, as well as "flocks" on 25th July 1957.

Baxter and Rintoul (Birds of Scotland, 1953) stated it was breeding at Inchkeith.

Cameron stated that it bred every year from 1954 and very likely previous to that. Thirty-eight nests with young were counted in 1960. All the nests at that time were located in old army huts, but many of these sites have disappeared.

Nevertheless, the common starling has probably continued to breed every year since. In 1994 a minimum of four nest sites were identified and starlings were undoubtedly breeding in 1996. On 25th May 1997 at least three birds flew from nesting holes where they were feeding young.

Cameron reported the common starling as present all the year round, with birds roosting in the old buildings. In January 1958 he estimated that not more that 150 were roosting on the island and perhaps less than 100 were doing this at the end of 1960. Flocks of between twenty and seventy are sometimes witnessed during visits to the island.

COMMON LINNET *Carduelis cannabina*

Baxter and Rintoul (Vertebrate Fauna of Forth, 1935) stated that one or two pairs bred in 1912 and that there were occasionally big flocks in October.

Common linnets were present in June 1934 and 1936 and up to sixteen were seen at any one time between 17th September and 16th October 1939. On 6th July 1951 Sandeman found them to be "plentiful in family parties".

Cameron also found them to be most common in autumn, when up to fifty were present. Single nests were found in 1958 and 1959 and in 1960, at least eight pairs bred. Small numbers have been recorded during most breeding seasons since and an occasional nest has been found.

Five old nests were discovered in a large clump of elder in 1994, along with a fresh nest containing five eggs.

On 10th June 1995 one pair of birds were present. Also four nests were found in the same elder patch as the 1994 record. Two of these nests were old, whilst a third nest contained an addled egg, and the fourth contained a sizeable, dead chick.

An individual bird was seen on 6th May 1996. Out-with the breeding season, an individual was recorded on 4th January 1984 and at least fifteen were present on 15th November 2002.

REED BUNTING *Emberiza schoeniclus*

A male bird was recorded at the island on 16th June 1934, and a pair with newly fledged young were witnessed on 28th July 1955. However, Cameron did not record the reed bunting during his time at Inchkeith.

Three pairs bred in 1968 and a nest containing five chicks was discovered in 1969. The reed bunting was recorded at the island during the breeding season of most years between 1971 and 1977 (usually only one bird, but two in 1975). It was not seen again until 20th June 1988, when a male bird was sighted.

HOUSE SPARROW *Passer domesticus*

The house sparrow was recorded in June 1934 and 1936 and was seen regularly between 17th September and 19th November 1939. It was present in July 1951 and a flock was observed in August of that year.

Cameron recorded the house sparrow as breeding every year between 1957-60, with an estimated seven pairs nesting in the latter year. He often noted between fifteen to twenty birds present in the autumn, but only saw the house sparrow occasionally during mid-winter.

From Cameron's time, until 1975, the house sparrow was still occasionally recorded during the breeding season. This species often follows man to remote locations, and likewise deserts these places if the human presence ceases. Inchkeith is now uninhabited and it appears the house sparrow has abandoned the island as a breeding place, as it has not been recorded from the island for quite some time.

GREAT CORMORANT

LIST OF NON-BREEDING BIRDS RECORDED FROM INCHKEITH

This section deals with non-breeding and migrant birds recorded at, or from, Inchkeith. Much has yet to be learned about the current usage of the island by birds during the winter months and what Baxter and Rintoul, and Cameron found in their times, need not necessarily be the case today.

One hundred and one species are quoted in this section but, because this total has been compiled from only a few diverse references, the true figure of bird species which have visited the island must be much higher.

Black-throated Diver	Whimbrel	Mistle Thrush
Great Northern Diver	Bar-tailed Godwit	Fieldfare
Red-throated Diver	Common Sandpiper	Redwing
Great Crested Grebe	Common Redshank	Northern Wheatear
Red-necked Grebe	Red Knot	Stonechat
Slavonian Grebe	Purple Sandpiper	Whinchat
Black-necked Grebe	Dunlin	Common Redstart
European Storm-petrel	Red-necked Phalarope	Sedge Warbler
Manx Shearwater	Great Skua	Blackcap
Sooty Shearwater	Arctic Skua	Garden Warbler
Northern Gannet	Pomarine Skua	Common Whitethroat
Grey Heron	Long-tailed Skua	Willow Warbler
Eurasian Wigeon	Mew Gull	Common Chiffchaff
Northern Shoveler	Little Gull	Wood Warbler
Greater Scaup	Black-headed Gull	Goldcrest
Tufted Duck	Common Tern	Spotted Flycatcher
Long-tailed Duck	Arctic Tern	Pied Flycatcher
Velvet Scoter	Roseate Tern	Pied Wagtail
Black Scoter	Little Tern	Yellow Wagtail
Red-breasted Merganser	Sandwich Tern	Bohemian Waxwing
Smew	Little Auk	European Greenfinch
Brent Goose	Black Guillemot	Eurasian Siskin
Mute Swan	Common Wood Pigeon	European Goldfinch
Common Buzzard	European Turtle Dove	Twite
Peregrine Falcon	Common Cuckoo	CommonRedpoll

LIST OF NON-BREEDING BIRDS RECORDED FROM INCHKEITH (CONTINUED)

Eurasian Sparrowhawk
Common Kestrel
Black Grouse
Corn Crake
Northern Lapwing
Common Raven
Ruddy Turnstone
Eurasian Jackdaw
Eurasian Curlew

Long-eared Owl
Short-eared Owl
Common Swift
House Martin
Sand Martin
Grey Plover
Rook
Eurasian Woodcock
Coal Tit

Chaffinch
Brambling
Yellow Hammer
Snow Bunting
Ringed Plover
Hooded Crow
Common Snipe
Blue Tit

GATHERING OF ATLANTIC PUFFINS

HISTORICAL DETAILS OF NON-BREEDING BIRDS RECORDED FROM INCHKEITH

BLACK-THROATED DIVER   *Gavia arctica*
Baxter and Rintoul had several records of black-throated diver being seen off the island (Vertebrate Fauna of Forth, 1935). The only subsequent record is of a single bird on 11th January 1960.

GREAT NORTHERN DIVER   *Gavia immer*
Dr. Sibbald recorded in 1684, that a great northern diver was killed by a bullet off the island of Keith (i.e. Inchkeith). Thirteen were off the island on 10th November 1911 and more were seen five days later.

RED-THROATED DIVER   *Gavia stellata*
Baxter and Rintoul (Vertebrate Fauna of Forth, 1935) stated red-throated diver had been seen in April. Since 1957 there have been several infrequent records of individuals in January, February, June and October. Two were seen on 4th June 1976, four on 4th January 1984, and three on 15th November 2002.

GREAT CRESTED GREBE   *Podiceps cristatus*
One bird was recorded on 14th -15th February 1960

RED-NECKED GREBE   *Podiceps grisegena*
Individual birds were recorded on 9th February 1912, 12th October 1939, 27th September 1957, 28th February and 24th - 26th October 1960, and 4th January 1984.

SLAVONIAN GREBE   *Podiceps auritus*
One "probable" record of a bird on 2nd - 4th January 1960.

BLACK-NECKED GREBE   *Podiceps nigricollis*
One bird was recorded on 25th December 1939.

EUROPEAN STORM-PETREL   *Hydrobates pelagicus*
Two birds were observed close inshore during the summer of 1913. Baxter and Rintoul thought this to be interesting, and suggested the possibility of breeding. N.B. a breeding attempt was made at Bass Rock in 1904.

MANX SHEARWATER   *Puffinus puffinus*
Baxter and Rintoul (Vertebrate Fauna of Forth, 1935) found them as far up the Firth as Inchkeith during the summer months and hoped it would not be long before they were found nesting. Individual birds and flocks of up to fifty have been recorded regularly between April and October. At least fifty birds were recorded on 8th July 1995 flying northwards about half to one mile west of Inchkeith. A further five birds were recorded off the island on 2nd June 1996.

SOOTY SHEARWATER   *Puffinus griseus*
One record exists of a bird near the island on 22nd September 1911.
NORTHERN GANNET   *Morus bassanus*
Seen regularly offshore from March to November. Occurs most often in September following the peak movement of juveniles from the Bass Rock. Two records exist of dead birds from the island, a juvenile on 21st October 1960 and an adult on 18th July 1975.
GREY HERON   *Ardea cinerea*
Five records exist. Three birds flying south on 31st August 1960, one bird present on 16th June 1968, one bird on 6th November 1995, another individual on 10th November 2001 and two on 15th November 2002.
EURASIAN WIGEON   *Anas penelope*
Two records exist. One of ten birds on 6th May 1914 and one of eight birds on 2nd October 1939.
NORTHERN SHOVELER   *Anas clypeata*
One bird was recorded on 22nd February 1914 and one (same bird?) was at the lighthouse lantern on 28th February 1914.
GREATER SCAUP   *Aythya marila*
A single duck was noted on 14th January 1960 and "flights" of scaup were recorded on 6th and 25th January 1940.
TUFTED DUCK   *Aythya fuligula*
This species was recorded on 5th and 11th November 1912.
LONG-TAILED DUCK   *Clangula hyemalis*
Three records exist. Two birds on 18th December 1939, one on 16th February 1960 and one on 4th January 1984.
VELVET SCOTER   *Melanitta fusca*
Nine birds were recorded on 29th November 1939.
BLACK SCOTER   *Melanitta nigra*
Three records exist. One bird was recorded on 18th December 1939, another on 16th February 1960 and ninety were flying near the island on 30th June 1965.
RED-BREASTED MERGANSER   *Mergus serrator*
Cameron recorded small numbers, not exceeding eleven, fairly regularly during January to March. Between 12th-14th January 1960 he counted twenty, twenty-three and forty-two respectively. He also noted one bird on 30th October 1960. Two were recorded on 4th January 1984, and four drakes flew near the harbour area on 6th June 1993.

COMMON EIDER DUCK

GREAT CORMORANT COLONY

BLACK-LEGGED KITTIWAKES

HERRING GULL

GREY SEAL COW & PUP

GREY SEAL PUP

SCARLET PIMPERNEL

HENBANE

SMEW   *Mergus albellus*
A drake and a duck were recorded on 20th December 1912.
BRENT GOOSE   *Branta bernicla*
A probable record of fifteen - twenty of the dark bellied phase of this species was made on 31st December 1958. They were flying south-south-eastwards.
MUTE SWAN   *Cygnus olor*
Five records exist. Two birds were present on 7th October 1939, one on 31st May 1958, three on 10th February 1959, three on 26th January 1960 and a single immature bird on 15th November 2002. The 1958, 1959 and 1960 records all occurred during foggy weather.
COMMON BUZZARD   *Buteo buteo*
One bird was recorded on 13th January 1959. Another was seen flying over the north- east end of the island on 15th November 2002.
PEREGRINE FALCON   *Falco peregrinus*
One bird seen on 18th December 1960. In recent times peregrines are believed to have visited Inchkeith during the autumn and winter months from the Fife mainland. A female bird was present on 10th November 2001 and at least one male was recorded on 15th November 2002.
EURASIAN SPARROWHAWK   *Accipiter nisus*
Two records exist. A single bird was seen on 9th September 1989 and another (probably a male) was recorded on 6th November 1995.
COMMON KESTREL   *Falco tinnunculus*
First recorded in the autumn of 1912. Since then it has been seen many times, mainly from July - March. Between 1978 and 1989, up to three birds occasionally remained at the island for periods during the winter months. Individual birds were witnessed hovering over the island on 23rd September 1997 and 10th November 2001 and two were present on 15th November 2002.
BLACK GROUSE   *Tetrao tetrix*
A female (grey hen) appeared at the island on 4th May 1913 and remained for one month.
CORN CRAKE   *Crex crex*
This species was heard calling on several successive nights during the autumn of 1956. One bird was present for over ten days in June 1968, and was seen at the end of the month. Another individual was present in May 1971 and three birds were heard calling all night in June 1980.
NORTHERN LAPWING   *Vanellus vanellus*
Baxter and Rintoul (Vertebrate Fauna of Forth, 1935) stated this species was occasionally seen on passage. Other records are of two on 20th June 1957, eight on 28th March, seven on 29th -30th March, and three on 18th April 1958. On 9th

February 1959 birds were heard calling during thick fog, and a single bird was seen on 3rd June. Six were recorded on 28th February 1960.

RINGED PLOVER *Charadrius hiaticula*

One record exists of six birds on 2nd May 1994.

GREY PLOVER *Pluvialis squatarola*

One record exists of a single bird on 4th January 1984.

RUDDY TURNSTONE *Arenaria interpres*

The ruddy turnstone's main passage months are March - April and October-November, but it occurs at Inchkeith during all months of the year. Cameron regularly recorded flocks of between twenty - fifty birds during all months, except June and July when he saw them only occasionally in twos and threes. He had noted flocks of between 180 - 200 in every month from October to early May and during very stormy weather on 24th October 1960, he recorded a flock of 300 birds. There have been a number of records since, including sixty-three on 3rd May 1993, twenty-four on 6th May 1996, 100 + on 10th November 2001 and ten on 15th November 2002.

COMMON SNIPE *Gallinago gallinago*

There are five records, all of individuals, occurring on 21st January and 20th February 1958 and 21st February, 6th and 13th March 1960.

EURASIAN WOODCOCK *Scolopax rusticola*

One bird was recorded on 30th March 1958, and one on each of the dates, 7th, 11th, 13th and 17th January 1959 (probably the same bird).

EURASIAN CURLEW *Numenius arquata*

Recorded in every month of the year. Highest figures noted are twenty-six on 6th September 1959, thirty on 4th January 1984, twenty-nine on 6th November 1995, over twenty on 10th November 2001 and about forty on 15th November 2002.

WHIMBREL *Numenius phaeopus*

First recorded in May 1914. Five were present on 2nd August 1951. Cameron recorded it each year on autumn passage between 16th July and 10th September, but on not more than six different days each autumn. One or two birds were present on each occasion, with three being noted on 20th August 1959, the most he saw at any one time. His only spring record is of two birds on 9th May 1958.

BAR-TAILED GODWIT *Limosa lapponica*

Between fifty and one hundred birds were present on 25th and 26th September 1939 and 500 were counted on 16th November that year.

COMMON SANDPIPER *Actitis hypoleucos*

One bird was present on 2nd August 1951, two on 30th August 1960 and one on 5th September of the same year.

COMMON REDSHANK   *Tringa totanus*
Cameron recorded it throughout the year except during the period 1st May to 24th June. Less than ten birds were seen on most occasions, except during August - September when between ten and fifteen birds were noted on four occasions and, on 21st April 1960 he recorded a flock of eighteen birds.
Common redshank have been recorded on several occasions in more recent times, i.e. two on 4th January 1984, one on 17th June 1984, six on 2nd April 1990, one on 6th November 1995, two on 10th November 2001 and ten on 15th November 2002.

RED KNOT   *Calidris canutus*
Five records exist of single birds, on 8th September 1957, 21st March 1958, 11th February, 15th March and 19th December 1960. Eight birds were recorded on 19th October 1960 and 150 birds were present at Long Craig on 6th May 1996.

PURPLE SANDPIPER   *Calidris maritima*
The earliest records are of one bird on 23rd November 1911, and another on 30th July 1912. Sandeman recorded them on three occasions, i.e. ten on 2nd October, twenty on 12th October and four on 7th November 1939.
Cameron recorded it throughout the year, except between 19th May and 23rd July. He encountered the largest numbers between December and March, when flocks of twenty - forty were present and, on 10th March 1960 he recorded fifty-one birds.
More recent records are nineteen on 4th January 1984, twenty-eight on 3rd May 1993, ten on 2nd May 1994, four on 4th May 1998 and one on 15th November 2002.

DUNLIN   *Calidris alpina*
Cameron recorded it a few times during January and February, when he noted up to eighty birds present. He also recorded very small numbers during November and late April to early May.

RED-NECKED PHALAROPE   *Phalaropus lobatus*
One was shot in the Forth near Inchkeith on 4th December 1854 and on 9th June 1901 two were seen about one mile west of the island.

GREAT SKUA   *Catharacta skua*
Recorded on a number of occasions between 22nd September and 29th October 1939, usually single birds, but up to four seen at a time. Single birds also seen on 12th October 1958, 14th September and 20th October 1960.

ARCTIC SKUA   *Stercorarius parasiticus*
According to Baxter and Rintoul (Vertebrate Fauna of Forth, 1935) the arctic skua occurred frequently off Inchkeith. Single birds were recorded in September and October 1939, with four seen on 1st October. Cameron made a good many records from 23rd August to 31st October during his time at the island. This species appeared

to be more numerous in 1960 than in his previous years, especially during September when he frequently saw two or three and on 20th September he recorded five, the most he encountered in a single day. He had one November record of two birds occurring on 14th November 1957.

POMARINE SKUA   *Stercorarius pomarinus*
A single bird was recorded on 20th October 1960 during stormy weather.

LONG-TAILED SKUA   *Stercorarius longicaudus*
One bird was recorded as being near Inchkeith on 6th June 1913.

MEW GULL (Common Gull)   *Larus canus*
Dr. Sibbald (1710), stated the common sea-mall (common gull) frequented Inchkeith's shores. One bird was seen on 16th June 1934, two on 23rd September and two on 2nd October 1939. Cameron saw it occasionally during the autumn in very small numbers. Ten were recorded on 4th January 1984.

LITTLE GULL   *Larus minutus*
One probable immature bird was found washed up dead on 22nd February 1958.

BLACK-HEADED GULL   *Larus ridibundus*
Cameron recorded it as present around the island from about mid-July until early March. He found it occurred in small numbers at first, but numbers increased during September and from then until January up to 400 had been recorded, but numbers varied considerably. He also noticed a clear decrease in February. Black-headed gulls also appeared on passage during April-June. Thirty birds were recorded on 4th January 1984 and an individual bird likewise on 6th May 1996.

COMMON TERN   *Sterna hirundo*
Dr. Sibbald (1710) lists the "pictarne" (common tern) in a short list of those species which frequented Inchkeith's shores in his time. The next record is from 16th June 1934. Common terns were seen regularly from 17th September until 17th October 1939, with 100 present on 23rd September.

Cameron recorded "Commic" terns (i.e. Common or Arctic Terns) between 1st May and 25th October, throughout his stay. In August and September flights alighted at the southern tip of the island, with up to 700 and 1,000 being present in a day. More recently, a single bird was seen carrying a fish on 10th June 1995 and two were recorded on 8th July of the same year.

ARCTIC TERN   *Sterna paradisaea*
Only three definite records exist. Two birds were seen on 23rd and 25th September 1939. In more recent times, a single bird was seen feeding in the harbour area on 6th July 2002.

ROSEATE TERN *Sterna dougallii*
Two probable records exist for this species, one bird on 9th September and three birds on 13th September 1957.

LITTLE TERN *Sterna albifrons*
Cameron occasionally recorded one or two birds during September.

SANDWICH TERN *Sterna sandvicensis*
First recorded on 16th June 1934. It was further recorded between 17th - 26th September 1939.
Cameron noted it each year in August or September, usually in small numbers, with up to twenty birds on a few occasions. More recently, three were seen on 2nd May 1994, two on 10th June 1995 and one on 8th July 1995.

LITTLE AUK *Alle alle*
Two birds were witnessed off Inchkeith on 24th January 1940 and four were caught at the island the following day.
Dead birds were found washed ashore on 24th February and 15th November 1959, and also on 13th January 1960.

BLACK GUILLEMOT *Cepphus grylle*
An immature bird was seen near the pier on 15th June 1969 and an adult bird was recorded offshore on 11th May 1974.

COMMON WOOD PIGEON *Columba palumbus*
Three records exist of single birds: on 20th January 1958, 12th June 1977 and 14th June 1981. On the latter two occasions the birds were seen flying from elder bushes, the nesting places for this species both on Cramond Island and Inchcolm. It is possible this species may have attempted breeding in the past.

EUROPEAN TURTLE DOVE *Streptopelia turtur*
A single bird was flushed from an elder bush near the harbour on 15th June 1997.

COMMON CUCKOO *Cuculus canorus*
One was present during the forenoon of 1st May 1957.

LONG-EARED OWL *Asio otus*
One bird was present on 5th November 1958.

SHORT-EARED OWL *Asio flammeus*
Cameron recorded single birds on up to four occasions during September - October, during each year of his stay. Four birds stayed for several weeks during the winter of 1979 - 80 and two owls, probably of this species, over-wintered in 1988 - 89.

COMMON SWIFT *Apus apus*
Assemblies were seen over Inchkeith (probably hawking for insects) on 2nd June 1912 and 13th June 1914. One was killed at the lighthouse lantern on 2nd May

1913 and another was seen on 16th September 1913. Two were recorded on 27th - 28th June 1936.

Cameron's earliest record in the year is of two birds on 16th May (1959) and his latest record is of a single bird on 23rd September (1957). He saw them occasionally during June, July and August with most records occurring in July, usually of less than ten birds. The largest movement he recorded was on 5th July 1960 during a day of thick, foggy rain, when flocks of up to ten birds were seen several times and, at 1745 hours, over forty were flying above the island.

On 6th June 1998 twenty-seven common swifts were recorded flying over the island, north to south.

HOUSE MARTIN   *Delichon urbica*

Occurred on passage in May 1913. One bird was recorded on 13th May 1959 and three on 16th May.

SAND MARTIN   *Riparia riparia*

Occurred in some numbers on 4th June 1912.

COMMON RAVEN   *Corvus corax*

One bird was at the island on 2nd March 1914.

CROW (Hooded Crow sub-species)   *Corvus corone cornix*

Records exist of single birds on 1st November 1959 and 31st October 1960. On 21st October 1960 five were seen feeding on a dead immature gannet.

ROOK   *Corvus frugilegus*

According to Baxter and Rintoul (Vertebrate Fauna of Forth, 1935) the rook was occasionally seen on passage. Five birds were recorded on 25th September 1959, four on 23rd March and one on 17th April 1960, all flying southwards. Dead immatures were found on 10th and 12th April 1960.

EURASIAN JACKDAW   *Corvus monedula*

Two birds were recorded on 3rd October 1957 and another two on 4th March 1959. An immature was found dead on 12th June 1966.

BLUE TIT   *Parus caeruleus*

One bird was present on 24th October 1957.

COAL TIT   *Parus ater*

One bird was present on 30th April 1958.

MISTLE THRUSH   *Turdus viscivorus*

Only recorded in 1958, once in April and three times in November, with three being the most birds seen in a day.

FIELDFARE   *Turdus pilaris*
Baxter and Rintoul (Vertebrate Fauna of Forth, 1935) have it recorded on migration. Cameron recorded it from October through to March. There was some passage in October, but he made few records for the other months, and there were never more than seven present, except during thick weather on 26th October 1960 when there was a flock of at least 150 Turdidae over the island, the majority being Fieldfares. This was an unusually large passage for the island.

REDWING   *Turdus iliacus*
Redwings were included in a movement of thrushes on 5th November 1939. Cameron recorded it as a bird of passage in small numbers during October with not more than twelve birds at a time. He also noted mostly single birds on a few occasions during November, January and February.

NORTHERN WHEATEAR   *Oenanthe oenanthe*
Baxter and Rintoul (Vertebrate Fauna of Forth, 1935) recorded the northern wheatear as a bird of double passage on Isle of May, Inchkeith, and Bass Rock, sometimes in considerable numbers, passing in spring between 21st March and 10th June and in autumn between 6th July and mid October, with stragglers up to 1st November.

Cameron also found it was a bird of double passage, in spring between 30th March to 10th May and in autumn from 7th July to 27th September. He also noted a steady regular passage of small numbers in autumn, of not more that five in a day.

STONECHAT   *Saxicola torquata*
A female bird was recorded on 24th March 1913 and another bird was seen on 1st March 1959.

WHINCHAT   *Saxicola rubetra*
Baxter and Rintoul (Vertebrate Fauna of Forth, 1935) had many records of whinchats on passage at Inchkeith. In spring they occurred between 25th April and the end of May and in autumn from mid - August to the first week of October. Cameron sighted very few birds (all singles) during August or September.

COMMON REDSTART   *Phoenicurus phoenicurus*
Single birds were recorded on 4th, 5th, and 6th September 1958 and on 14th, 15th May 1960. Three birds were seen on 17th September, followed by five on 18th September 1960.

SEDGE WARBLER   *Acrocephalus schoenobaenus*
Two birds were recorded on 2nd September 1914. Baxter and Rintoul (Birds of Scotland, 1953) stated it was bird of double passage at Inchkeith. Cameron recorded individuals on 2nd September 1958, 10th and 28th August 1959 and two on 22nd August 1959. There is a further record of an individual on 11th May 1974.

BLACKCAP *Sylvia atricapilla*

Blackcaps were killed at the lighthouse lantern on 1st and 9th November 1913. Baxter and Rintoul (Birds of Scotland, 1953) stated it has occurred on passage, but not in any great numbers. There is a "probable" record of a bird on 14th May 1958 and another of a bird on 29th October 1960.

GARDEN WARBLER *Sylvia borin*

One struck the lighthouse lantern on 27th September 1913. Baxter and Rintoul (Birds of Scotland, 1953) stated it has occurred on passage. Single birds were recorded on 2nd September 1958 and 10th May 1959 (at the lighthouse lantern) and two were seen on 17th September 1960.

COMMON WHITETHROAT *Sylvia communis*

Baxter and Rintoul (Vertebrate Fauna of Forth, 1935) stated it was one of the commonest passage migrants on the Forth islands and had records of it from Inchkeith. The periods of movement quoted are, from the latter end of April throughout May, occasionally in early June, and from mid-August to mid-October. There are three records of single birds, i.e. 22nd August 1959 and 19th August and 15th September 1960.

WILLOW WARBLER *Phylloscopus trochilus*

Willow warblers are said to have been "swarming" on Inchkeith on 16th August 1913. Baxter and Rintoul had other records for the island and in "Birds of Scotland" stated it was a bird of double passage at Inchkeith.

Cameron also found it to be a bird of double passage, with small numbers appearing between 16th April and 26th May (at least thirteen on 14th May 1960 the highest spring total) and very small numbers between the second half of August up to 17th September. He recorded that on 2nd September 1958, "many" were present throughout the island, and gave a figure of twenty-three for 22nd August 1959.

At least six were present on 14th May 1978, three on 2nd May 1994, another six on 6th May 1996 and a pair on 4th May 1998.

COMMON CHIFFCHAFF *Phylloscopus collybita*

One bird, which was probably of this species, was noted on 1st May 1958, and another was recorded on 22nd August 1959. Both birds were caught at the lighthouse lantern.

WOOD WARBLER *Phylloscopus sibilatrix*

Two "probable" wood warblers were recorded on 22nd August 1959.

GOLDCREST *Regulus regulus*

Baxter and Rintoul (Vertebrate Fauna of Forth, 1935) stated it was recorded on double passage at Inchkeith lighthouse. Cameron also found the goldcrest to be a bird of double passage, but in small numbers of up to seven. It occurred very

occasionally between 23rd March and 21st April and more regularly during September and October. He also stated that few birds came to the lighthouse lantern, but more goldcrests have been found there than all other species together.
There is a more recent record of a single bird at the island on 2nd April 1990.

SPOTTED FLYCATCHER　　*Muscicapa striata*

There is one record of a single bird on 17th September 1960.

PIED FLYCATCHER　　*Ficedula hypoleuca*

According to Baxter and Rintoul (Vertebrate Fauna of Forth, 1935) the pied flycatcher had occurred at Inchkeith. Cameron recorded individuals on 22nd August 1959 and 17th September 1960. On 18th June 1967 a male bird which had been dead for several weeks was found within a hole in a building.

PIED WAGTAIL　　*Motacilla alba*

Baxter and Rintoul (Vertebrate Fauna of Forth, 1935) stated the pied wagtail was seen on passage at Inchkeith.

Two "white" wagtails (*Motacilla alba alba*) visited the island on 5th April 1914. Between two and twelve pied wagtails were recorded between 17th September and 17th October 1939. Cameron recorded "alba" Wagtails very occasionally, with up to seven at a time during August, September and October and single birds once in both April and June. Two pied wagtails were present on 14th May 1978. More recent records are: one bird on 10th June 1995, up to three on 6th May 1996, two on 25th May and 15th June 1997 and one on 2nd June 2001.

YELLOW WAGTAIL　　*Motacilla flava*

Cameron noted a "flava" wagtail on 8th September 1958 and thought it was a yellow wagtail.

BOHEMIAN WAXWING　　*Bombycilla garrulus*

One was recorded on 5th February 1959.

EUROPEAN GREENFINCH　　*Carduelis chloris*

Baxter and Rintoul (Vertebrate Fauna of Forth, 1935) have it recorded as a bird of double passage, and that thirty to forty were at the island on 1st December 1913. Between four and six were present between 17th September and 19th November 1939. Cameron saw small parties of up to fifteen birds quite regularly during the winter months. He also saw them on rare occasions in May and September. A dead bird was found on 18th June 1978 and two males were present on 18th May 1975.

EURASIAN SISKIN　　*Carduelis spinus*

According to Baxter and Rintoul (Vertebrate Fauna of Forth, 1935) large flocks were seen on passage in the autumn, and smaller numbers occurred in the spring. Cameron only made a single record, of one bird, on 17th September 1960. However, a flock of about forty eurasian siskins was recorded on 10th November 2001.

EUROPEAN GOLDFINCH *Carduelis carduelis*
Three birds were recorded on 15th November 2002.
TWITE *Carduelis flavirostris*
Twenty birds were present on 14th January and ten on 20th January 1960.
COMMON REDPOLL *Carduelis flammea*
One was caught at the lighthouse lantern on 7th November 1959.
CHAFFINCH *Fringilla coelebs*
According to Baxter and Rintoul (Vertebrate Fauna of Forth, 1935) chaffinches appeared in large numbers during the autumn, and again during the spring migration, but in lesser numbers. Cameron encountered it occasionally from October to March in very small numbers, of up to ten at a time.
BRAMBLING *Fringilla montifringilla*
Baxter and Rintoul (Vertebrate Fauna of Forth, 1935) stated bramblings have occurred on passage at Inchkeith. The only subsequent record is of three birds recorded on 20th February 1960.
YELLOWHAMMER *Emberiza citrinella*
A female bird was recorded on 12th May 1912. Another bird occurred on 22nd October 1958 and a third was present between 20th - 23rd October 1960.
SNOW BUNTING *Plectrophenax nivalis*
Baxter and Rintoul (Vertebrate Fauna of Forth, 1935) stated they had several records of its passage in autumn. A small party of up to six birds were present on 9th February 1959 and a single bird was recorded on 4th, 5th and 7th November in the same year.

LESSER BLACK-BACKED GULL CHICKS

MAMMALS

Other than domesticated animals, which have been introduced to Inchkeith on a number of occasions over the centuries, only five mammal species have been recorded from the island. These are: the grey seal, common seal, rabbit, brown rat, and house mouse. All of these still occur at the island, although information about the brown rat's current status is sketchy.

The three terrestrial species were all introduced by man. In the case of the rabbit, introduction was deliberate, whilst the brown rat and house mouse, were introduced accidentally. It is possible the brown rat was preceded by the black rat, and subsequently displaced that species.

Records for all the aforementioned species are scarce, but the following notes are sufficient for an insight into this aspect of the island's natural history. There are no domestic animals currently on Inchkeith.

GREY SEAL   *Halychoerus grypus*

Few records exist from the past in relation to seals occurring at Inchkeith, and most of those which do, refer only to "seals", making it impossible to be certain as to which of our two seal species is being referred to.

Dr. Sibbald (1710) only recorded the common seal as frequenting the Firth of Forth in his time and also said they were to be found at the isles. However, the occurrence of the grey seal at, or near Inchkeith, at other times can be assumed from the results of an investigation of an ancient kitchen midden on the island in 1870, when the bones of the grey seal were discovered along with the bones of several domesticated animals and rabbits. This tends to show that at one time the island's inhabitants caught seals as a source of food and fur.

One record from the early part of the 19th century states that as many as seventy seals were counted at Inchkeith during the winter time and, judging from the time of year, these may well have been grey seals visiting the island at pupping time, or merely a displacement of common seals from the Kinghorn area due to human predation.

A further reference from 1857 also states "seals" occurred at the island.

However, in 1872 the grey seal was reported to be extinct in the Firth of Forth and, by the end of the 19th century, sightings of grey seals were so rare in the estuary that they merited a mention in local newspapers.

Since about the middle of the 20th century grey seals have become increasingly more common in the Forth, and during the last two or three decades this has been reflected by their increased presence at Inchkeith.

However, it has only been during the last few years that any attempt has been made to assess the actual numbers of seals occurring at the island. More than twenty-two grey seals were recorded basking on the island's offshore rocks on 6th June 1993. On 2nd May the following year twenty-three were present and a few weeks later, on 10th June thirty-five were noted.

Up to thirty-four were present on 8th July 1995 at Iron Craig, a small reef off the south-west corner of Inchkeith. This reef appears to be one of the grey seal's favourite hauling out places at the island when the tidal conditions are right. Over fifty-five grey seals were recorded on 6th May 1996, most of which were at Iron Craig. This number is the peak count to date. Twenty animals were hauled out at the same location on 15th June 1997, at least eighteen on 29th June and about twelve on 6th July 2002.

Early in the 1990's it was suspected that a small number of grey seal pups were being born at Inchkeith during the autumn months. A visit to the island on 17th November 1994 confirmed the presence of two recently born pups. On 6th November the following year a single pup was recorded at the north end of the island and four recently weaned pups were observed on Seal Carr, a small reef off the island's west side. Twenty-six adult grey seals were also counted on the same date. The newly weaned pups may have come from the large colony at May Island rather than having been born on Inchkeith.

It is believed the number of grey seal pups born at Inchkeith rose sharply during the pupping season of 2000 and may have numbered about two dozen. The island was visited on 10th November 2001 to establish an up to date status of the colony. During the visit twenty-seven pups and forty adults were counted, most of which were found at the southern end of the island. However, a similar trip on 15th November 2002 returned only eighteen pups and thirty-three adults.

COMMON SEAL *Phoca vitulina*

In the 12th century King David I granted a charter to the monastery of Dunfermline bestowing the monks every seventh seal caught at Kinghorn, after his own tithe had been set aside. This charter does not make any distinction between the common and the grey seal, but it is believed to refer to the common seal.

Although Dr. Sibbald (1710) stated only the common seal was found in the Forth, and at the isles, he did not specify the islands by name, but most likely he was including Inchkeith.

Nowadays both the common and grey seal are commonly found in the area of Kinghorn, with established colonies at the rocks adjacent to Seafield Tower, midway between Kinghorn and Kirkcaldy.

Undoubtedly common seals have visited Inchkeith's rocks in the past, but recent surveys tend to indicate the island is less agreeable to the common seal than the grey seal.

One - two animals were present at the island on 6th June 1993 and on 10th June the following year a further individual was recorded. Considerably more grey seals were counted at the island on both these dates. The common seal has not been recorded at Inchkeith since, but no doubt has occurred.

BROWN RAT   *Rattus norvegicus*

It has been speculated that brown rats did not reach the ports in the Firth of Forth until round about the middle of the 18th century. However, Sibbald in his "History of Fife and Kinross" (1710), states in reference to Inchkeith, "some rats from the ships have much increased". If the former statement is true, then Sibbald may have been referring to black rats (*rattus rattus*) which have been with us far longer than the brown rat.

Baxter and Rintoul (Vertebrate Fauna of Forth, 1935) stated "brown rats continue to inhabit this island (Inchkeith)."

If black rats ever colonised Inchkeith it seems they must have been displaced at some later time by the larger brown rat.

The current status of the brown rat is unclear as there has been an absence of confirmed live sightings for many years. Several possible sightings have been made in recent years, but in each case the observers could not make a categoric claim.

During a count of gull nests on 27th May 1994 two dead "rats" were found and although these could have been brought over to the island from rubbish tips by gulls, it is far more likely they originated from the island.

HOUSE MOUSE   *Mus musculus*

Baxter and Rintoul (Vertebrate Fauna of Forth, 1935) stated house mice were "very numerous on Inchkeith," and this appears to be their status today.

In recent times they have occasionally been encountered inside some of the old military buildings. A nest containing about six house mice was discovered inside a puffin burrow at the south end of the island on 15th November 2002 and, on the same date, another two house mice were observed on the path leading up from the harbour.

It is unknown when they first appeared at the island, but as with the brown rat they must have arrived by "assisted passage" at some stage.

RABBIT   *Onyctolagus cuniculus*

Rabbit bones were found in an ancient kitchen midden on Inchkeith during the early 1870's, suggesting rabbits were at one time farmed on the island as a source of food and fur. Exactly when they were introduced to Inchkeith is unknown, but as the animal is believed to have been brought to the country round about the beginning of the 12th century, its arrival at the island must have occurred at some time after that.

In the 16th century, Boece said the islands in the Forth were "verie full on conies" and he most likely included Inchkeith in this statement.

Several records exist in relation to rabbits occurring at Inchkeith during the 19th century. From the statistical account of 1845 we learn there were many rabbits on the island then and David Grieve, F.S.A. Scot, in his 1872 report on the kitchen midden stated; "the rabbit burrows, and is in a wild state".

In the years following Grieve's visit the island was purchased by the military and built up considerably during the latter part of the 19th century, and early years of the 20th century, with many fortifications and their associated buildings, and roads.

The rabbit appears to have died out during this period due to the presence of workmen, troops and dogs, which gave them little chance of survival.

However, in recent times the rabbit has re-appeared at Inchkeith. A small number are believed to have been introduced during the latter part of 1988 and the rabbit has been seen every year since, with over twelve individuals being recorded on 10th November 2001.

GREY SEAL PUP

BUTTERFLIES

The following brief list of butterflies recorded from Inchkeith has been compiled from occasional sightings noted by R.W.J. Smith and R. Morris during annual seabird counts, between the years 1979 and 2002.

So far only eight species have been recorded, and clearly this leaves ample scope for future additions.

Currently no records exist in respect of the island's moth populations.

Pieridae

LARGE WHITE   *Pieris brassicae*
Recorded in June 2002.
SMALL WHITE   *Pieris rapae*
Recorded in June 1993, possibly in July 1995, May 1997 and June 2002.
GREEN-VEINED WHITE   *Pieris napi*
Recorded in June 1979, 1980, 1981, May 1982, June 1988, possibly July 1995, May 1997 and June 2002.

Nymphalidae

SMALL TORTOISESHELL   *Aglais urticae*
Recorded in May and June 1993, June and July 1995, May and July 1996, May 1997, May 1998 and June 2002. On 15th November 2002 a single butterfly was found hibernating within the old military buildings at the south end of the island.
RED ADMIRAL   *Vanessa atalanta*
Recorded in June 1992 and 1993, July 1996, May 1997, May 1998 and June 2002.
PAINTED LADY   *Cynthia cardui*
Recorded in June 1980.

Lycaenidae

SMALL COPPER   *Lycaena phlaeas*
Recorded in June 1979 and 1981, May 1982 and June 1988
COMMON BLUE   *Polyommatus icarus*
Recorded in June 1980 and June 1988.

FLORA

Due to Inchkeith's exposed location in the middle of the Firth of Forth, the island is devoid of trees, except for a few examples of Elder, which grow in a few places, usually where they are afforded some form of shelter.

The island has for the most part, a thin covering of soil but nevertheless its seventy or so acres have provided good pasturage in the past for horses, cattle and sheep.

During the 16th century Scots troops, garrisoned at Leith, kept their horses on Inchkeith. It is said they were safer on the island (from the English) than on Leith Links, but another reason for putting them on the island was the reported high quality of the grass, which was said to be good for fattening horses. This arrangement led to the Scots' French allies naming Inchkeith, "L'ile des Chevaux", or "Island of Horses".

When Dr. Samuel Johnson and James Boswell Esq. visited Inchkeith in August 1773, at the beginning of their tour to the Hebrides, they found sixteen head of black cattle grazing upon it. No person was staying on the island at that time and the island was used only for summer grazing. They also noticed a profusion of thistles and nettles growing on the island.

Less than half a century later Thomas Carlyle made a similar visit to Inchkeith. This was thirteen years after the lighthouse was built (1804). He observed the grass to be mostly wild and scraggy, but equal to the keep of seven cows. There were also several small patches of weak, dishevelled barley, trying to grow under difficulties and a few square yards of potatoes equally ill off. These cattle and crops were obviously the property of the lightkeepers, kept in order to sustain themselves at their insular location.

At the end of the 19th century Dickson writing in "Emeralds Chased in Gold," stated Inchkeith "affords sufficient nutriment to a considerable number of sheep and cattle, and a few donkeys." He also remarked the flora was very varied and similar to that found on the adjoining mainland and other islands in the Forth and included the poisonous Henbane and *Sinapis nigra*, a species of black mustard, which was plentiful.

Dr. Sibbald (1710) has left us with the first list of plant species from the island, albeit a brief collection assembled in the form of a medicinal list; "It (Inchkeith) is fertile in plants, and produceth many wholesome herbs, such as the Dock, Tota Bona, Sorrel, Scabious, Wild Thime, Chickweed, *Papaver spumeum*, several sorts of Plantane, the Sea-pink, Scurvey-grass, Ground ivy, Dentelyon, *Sedum minimum*, the Burdock, *Senecio* or Groundswallow, Aparine, the Common Dock, Wild Germander, *Echium*, *Marrubium*, Henbane, and St. Mary's Thistle, sufficient for the care of diseases incident to those who dwell upon it".

From this reference we can deduce a small community lived on the island at that time and were most probably involved in fishing around the island's shores.

Domestic stock was kept on the island once more during the late 1980's, when the Allandale Animal Sanctuary moved to the island for a few short years. A horse, several ponies, a donkey, a herd of goats and a large pig, were all part of the charity's animals which were allowed the freedom of the island's pasturage.

These various periods of grazing, and no doubt there were many others, undoubtedly helped to influence the variety of flora found on the island. However, a greater influence must have taken place during the latter part of the 19th century, and early 20th century when the construction of fortifications, gun emplacements, associated buildings, roads and trenches, etc., completely transformed the face of the island. A considerable part of Inchkeith's flora must have been displaced by these works, but also in turn, opportunities would have arisen for other plant species to colonise. However, the absence of comprehensive records from the past makes it difficult to comment on what changes actually took place.

During the 1990's a considerable amount of soil erosion started to occur at the island, particularly on the steeper slopes, leaving bare patches of ground exposed to the elements for most of the year and also transforming large areas of grassland into "weed" beds. The likely reason for this change are a combination of factors; i.e. the presence of the island's large gull population during the summer months, with their dunging and nest building habits, causing damage to the vegetation; the steep slopes of the island being susceptible to erosion; generally thin layers of soil on top of Inchkeith's rock strata; and the exposed position of the island, which lies generally north to south, across the face of prevailing easterly and westerly winds, in the middle of the Firth.

These reasons receive further credence from the fact the island's gull population reached its peak round about the time the erosion became noticeable.

The first real attempt at documenting Inchkeith's flora took place in June 1966 when Elizabeth P. Beattie spent a few hours ashore for that purpose. Her findings are listed in the Transactions of the Botanical Society of Edinburgh (Vol.40, 1967, pages 251-257), but because of the limited time she spent on the island, her lists can hardly be expected to be complete, although they are extensive.

In June 1994 Douglas MacKean from the Royal Botanic Garden in Edinburgh, made a similar visit to Inchkeith for the purpose of expanding on Elizabeth P. Beattie's results. His findings, together with Beattie's lists, and several important records from the past, have been assembled by George Ballantyne (Fife's Botanical Recorder) into the following list, which is the most comprehensive list of flowering plants recorded from the island to date. No work appears to have been done on identifying the lower plants.

LIST OF FLORA RECORDED FROM INCHKEITH

Family and Botanical Name	Common Name
Pteropsida	
Athyrium filix-femina	Lady Fern
Dryopteris dilatata	Broad Buckler-fern
Dryopteris filix-mas	Male Fern
Ranunculaceae	
Ranunculus acris	Meadow Buttercup
Ranunculus ficaria	Lesser Celandine
Ranunculus repens	Creeping Buttercup
Ranunculus sardous	Hairy Buttercup
Brassicaceae (Cruciferae)	
Arabidopsis thaliana	Thale Cress
Brassica juncea	Chinese Mustard
Brassica napus	Rape
Brassica nigra	Black Mustard
Brassica oleracea	Wild Cabbage
Capsella bursa-pastoris	Shepherd's Purse
Cochlearia danica	Danish Scurvy-grass
Cochlearia officinalis	Common Scurvy-grass
Erysimum cheiri	Wallflower
Sisymbrium officinale	Hedge Mustard
Sisymbrium orientale	Eastern Rocket
Thlapsi arvense	Field Penny-cress
Resedaceae	
Reseda luteola	Weld
Violaceae	
Viola riviniana	Dog Violet
Carophyllaceae	
Arenaria serpyllifolia	Thyme-leaved Sandwort
Cerastium diffusum	Sea Mouse-ear
Cerastium fontanum	Common Mouse-ear

Family and Botanical Name	Common Name
Cerastium semidecandrum	Little Mouse-ear
Cerastium tomentosum	Snow-in-summer
Sagina maritima	Sea Pearlwort
Sagina procumbens	Procumbent Pearlwort
Silene latifolia	White Campion
Silene uniflora	Sea Campion
Spergularia marina	Lesser Sea-spurrey
Stellaria media	Chickweed
Chenopodiaceae	
Atriplex littoralis	Grass-leaved Orache
Atriplex patula	Common Orache
Atriplex prostrata	Spear-leaved Orache
Chenopodium bonus-henricus	Good King Henry
Malvaceae	
Malva sylvestris	Common Mallow
Lavatera arborea	Tree Mallow
Geraniaceae	
Erodium cicutarium	Common Stork's-bill
Geranium molle	Dove's-foot Crane's-bill
Fabaceae (Papilionaceae)	
Astragalus glycyphyllos	Wild Liquorice
Cytisus scoparius	Broom
Lathyrus pratensis	Meadow Vetchling
Lotus corniculatus	Bird's-foot Trefoil
Medicago lupulina	Black Medick
Ononis repens	Common Restharrow
Trifolium arvense	Hare's-foot Clover
Trifolium campestre	Hop Trefoil
Trifolium dubium	Lesser Trefoil
Trifolium hybridum	Alsike Clover
Trifolium ornithopodioides	Bird's-foot Clover
Trifolium pratense	Red Clover

Family and Botanical Name

Trifolium repens
Vicia cracca
Vicia hirsuta
Vicia sativa
  (sub-species "nigra")
Vicia sepium
Ulex europaeus
Rosaceae
Agrimonia eupatoria
Rubus latifolius
Rubus radula
Malus domestica
Potentilla anserina
Potentilla erecta
Potentilla neumanniana
Rosa canina
Crassulaceae
Sedum acre
Onagraceae
Chamerion angustifolium
Apiaceae (Umbelliferae)
Anthriscus caucalis
Conium maculatum
Heracleum sphondylium
Ligusticum scoticum
Oenanthe crocata
Petroselinum crispum
Polygonaceae
Rumex acetosa
Rumex crispus
Urticaceae
Urtica urens
Urtica dioica

Common Name

White Clover
Tufted Vetch
Hairy Tare
Narrow-leaved Vetch

Bush Vetch
Whin

Agrimony
Bramble
Bramble
Apple
Silverweed
Tormentil
Spring Cinquefoil
Common Dog Rose

Biting Stonecrop

Rosebay Willowherb

Bur Chervil
Hemlock
Hogweed
Scots' Lovage
Hemlock Water Dropwort
Garden Parsley

Common Sorrel
Curled Dock

Small Nettle
Common Nettle

Family and Botanical Name	Common Name
Juncaginaceae	
Triglochin maritima	Sea Arrow-grass
Plumbaginaceae	
Armeria maritima	Thrift; Sea Pink
Primulaceae	
Anagallis arvensis	Scarlet Pimpernel
Glaux maritima	Sea-Milkwort
Primula vulgaris	Primrose
Boraginaceae	
Anchusa arvensis	Lesser Bugloss
Echium vulgare	Viper's Bugloss
Myosotis arvensis	Field Forget-me-not
Myosotis discolor	Changing Forget-me-not
Solanaceae	
Hyoscyamus niger	Henbane
Scrophulariaceae	
Cymbalaria muralis	Ivy-leaved Toadflax
Euphrasia arctica	Eyebright
Linaria purpurea	Purple Toadflax
Veronica chamaedrys	Germander Speedwell
Lamiaceae (Labiatae)	
Glechoma hederacea	Ground-Ivy
Lamium purpureum	Red Dead-nettle
Marrubium vulgare	White Horehound
Thymus polytrichus	Wild Thyme
Plantaginaceae	
Plantago coronopus	Buck's-horn Plantain
Plantago lanceolata	Ribwort Plantain
Plantago major	Greater Plantain
Plantago maritima	Sea Plantain
Campanulaceae	
Campanula rotundifolia	Harebell (Scottish Bluebell)

Family and Botanical Name	Common Name
Rubiaceae	
Galium aparine	Sticky Willie
Galium verum	Lady's Bedstraw
Sherardia arvensis	Field Madder
Dipsaceae	
Knautia arvensis	Field Scabious
Caprifoliaceae	
Sambucus nigra	Elder
Compositae	
Achillea millefolium	Yarrow
Arctium minus	Burdock
Bellis perennis	Daisy
Centaura nigra	Common Knapweed
Cirsium arvense	Creeping Thistle
Cirsium vulgare	Spear Thistle
Carduus tenuiflorus	Slender Thistle
Pilosella officinarum	Mouse-ear Hawkweed
Senecio jacobaea	Common Ragwort
Senecio vulgaris	Groundsel
Silybum marianum	Milk Thistle
Sonchus oleraceus	Smooth Sow-thistle
Taraxacum officinale	Dandelion
Tripleurospermum inodorum	Scentless Mayweed
Tripleurospermum maritimum	Sea Mayweed
Liliaceae	
Hyacinthoides non-scriptus	Wild Hyacinth
Cyperaceae	
Carex distans	Distant Sedge
Carex otrubae	False Fox Sedge
Poaceae (Gramineae)	
Agrostis canina	Velvet Bent-grass
Agrostis capillaris	Common Bent-grass

Family and Botanical Name	Common Name
Agrostis stolonifera	Creeping Bent-grass
Aira caryophyllea	Silvery Hair-grass
Aira praecox	Early Hair-grass
Anisantha sterilis	Barren Brome
Anthoxanthum odoratum	Sweet Vernal Grass
Arrhenatherum elatius	False Oat-grass
Brachypodium sylvaticum	False Brome
Bromus hordeaceous	Soft Brome
Dactylis glomerata	Cock's-foot
Festuca arundinacea	Tall Fescue
Festuca rubra	Creeping Fescue
Helictotrichon pratense	Meadow Oat-grass
Helictotrichon pubescens	Downy Oat-grass
Holcus lanatus	Yorkshire-fog
Koeleria macrantha	Crested Hair-grass
Lolium perenne	Perennial Rye-grass
Poa annua	Annual Meadow-grass
Trisetum flavescens	Yellow Oat-grass

LESSER CELANDINE

EUROPEAN SHAG

COMMON EIDER DRAKES COURTING A FEMALE

SEA HUNTER

Skipper: Bill Simpson

Fishing Parties
Bird Watching
Diving Parties

Contact Bill on 07774 103405

It's Party Time Afloat

MAID OF THE FORTH

Apart from our regular Sealife cruises, our ferry service to lovely
Inchcolm Island and our popular
Evening Jazz Cruises.
You can charter the vessel for your own private Party!
Departures possible from Newhaven,
Tides Permitting

Whatever the celebration we have a range of packages available including catering and music options from a live band to Disco.

For Charter or Group Booking Enquiries Telephone Colin Aston on 01506 852296
24hr Sailing Infoline 0131 331 4857

NOTES